Short Stories for Christmas

Robert Parker

Published by Dolman Scott Ltd 2025

Copyright © 2025 Robert Parker

All rights reserved. No part of this publication may be reproduced, stored in a retrieval system, or transmitted in any form or by any means, electronic, mechanical, photocopy, recording or otherwise, without prior written permission of the copyright owner. Nor can it be circulated in any form of binding or cover other than that in which it is published and without similar condition including this condition being imposed on a subsequent purchaser.

ISBN: 978-1-915351-46-3

Published by
DolmanScott
www.dolmanscott.com

Short Stories for Christmas

Step into the warmth and wonder of Bethlehem in *Short Stories for Christmas* – a heart-warming collection of tales that reimagine the Nativity through the eyes of **animals, children, and unexpected heroes**.

A falcon guides Mary and Joseph with moonlight.
A donkey fetches firewood to warm the stable.
A mouse finds cheese to help make breakfast.
A magpie collects coins to help Joseph pay the innkeeper.
A sheep offers its wool to keep baby Jesus warm.

Each short story celebrates **kindness, generosity, and the spirit of Christmas**, showing how even the smallest creatures and acts of love can make a difference. Perfect for **families, children – and anyone who cherishes the magic of the holiday season**, this enchanting book brings new life to the most beloved Christmas story of all.

Join the journey, meet the animals, and discover the true meaning of Christmas!

Foreword

Do you have a favourite animal? And, if so, what is it about this animal that grabs your attention and interest? Do you have chance to interact with any of God's creatures? Perhaps you have one or more pets in your home. My own house is something of a menagerie, with a dog, a cat, and two rabbits. Happily, they all get along giving us much amusement and joy. We sometimes wonder what they make of us. Certainly, they look to us for affection, to play, for exercise, and most of all for food – indeed, our cat is masterful at convincing us that he's starving – when actually he's just been fed. Whilst I care about all of our animals, I have a particular soft spot for our dog, because she gives as well as takes. She shows us so much affection and instinctively knows when any of us needs a cuddle or hug.

In the short stories contained in this book you will meet lots of wonderful animals. You will see how each, in its own special way, played its part to help the holy family – that is the baby Jesus, Mary, and Joseph. You will also discover how this most important birth might have appeared from their point of view.

Christians believe that the gift of Jesus is the most special and important gift there could ever be. The Bible teaches us that this gift, the gift of God's own son, was not just to bring people back to God – but to save the whole world – to reveal God's love and care for every creature.

I am sure you will enjoy what follows. I hope that you will be inspired to care for all God's creatures, appreciating that they are valuable as we are. And I hope that through these stories we may be drawn to the baby at the heart of it all – discovering the love that has power to change us, and this world we share, for the better.

Nick Parker (Rector of St Alphege church, Solihull)

Table of Contents

Foreword v

Peter, the Peregrine Falcon 1

Dawnlight the Donkey Brings the Firewood 5

Excel the Eagle Brings the Fire 10

Caroline the Chicken's Special Gift 15

Mischief the Mouse Celebrates the Birth 18

Phantom the Fox and Felicity's Gift 23

Bluey the Blackbird Mends the Roof 27

Spinner the Spider Spins to Protect 33

Barry the Bat Clears the Air 37

Daniel the Canaan Dog Stands Guard 41

Casper the Cat Stands Watch 47

Candy the Cow Shares Her Milk 51

Surfinia the Sheep Gives Her Wool 57

Madge the Magpie Pays the Bill 61

Antwerp the Ass Announces the Birth 67

Daisychain the Duck Makes a Toy 71

The Visit of the Shepherds 76

The visit of the three kings,,, with gold and frankincense and myrrh 81

Slightly-Nightly the Nightingale Sings a Lullaby 87

Bundle-Some the Talking Budgie Warns the King 93

The Innkeeper Offers a Room 97

Sonia and the Precious Pearl 100

The Innkeeper's Wife Brings a Gift 105

Everybody Comes to the Stable 109

Wallie the Wolf Makes a Vow 113

Osbert the Wise Owl Watches Over the Stable 118

Homeward Bound 123

Cassidy the Cockerel Crows the Alarm... 126

Constance, Constantinople, and Canonfire: The Urgent Escape 131

Peter, the Peregrine Falcon

Joseph tugged gently on the donkey's rope.

"Halt," he said. The donkey, named Fergus, stopped right away. Mary, sitting on the donkey's back, looked around. The little town of Bethlehem was crowded, with people everywhere. They had been searching all evening for a place to stay.

"The inn across the street is our last chance," Joseph told Mary. "It's called 'Jerusalem Way,' but listen to all that noise inside. I think they'll tell me the same thing as the others: 'No room! We're full!'"

Just then, a sharp *Wark!* sounded from above. Joseph looked up and saw a bird sitting on the roof of the inn.

"A peregrine falcon?" Joseph said in surprise. "He shouldn't be here in town. He should be hunting out in the desert before it gets dark."

Mary gazed at the bird's shining eyes. "Look! He's staring at the moon, and his eyes are reflecting the light. They look like two little lanterns!" She smiled and called up to him, "Peter! Peter, come down! We won't hurt you."

The falcon didn't move.

"Birds are very careful," Joseph said. "I don't think he'll come. Stay here and keep an eye on Fergus while I check the inn. But don't get your hopes up – I'll probably be back with bad news."

Joseph disappeared inside. To Mary's surprise, he was back just a few minutes later, smiling.

"The innkeeper said there's no room inside, but when I told him you were about to have a baby, he offered us the stable out back," Joseph explained. "It's not far – just fifty metres away. We should find it easily, even in the dark."

Just then, another loud *"Wark!"* came from above. Peter the falcon took off from the roof, swooping down towards them.

Mary gasped. "Look at his eyes! He's using the moonlight to show us the way!"

Joseph laughed. "That's lucky! We might never have found the stable so quickly without Peter's help."

Soon, they arrived. The stable was simple, filled with straw and animals: cows, sheep, and a few chickens.

"It's not fancy, but it's warm," Joseph said. "Let's make a bed in the straw."

Mary smiled. "Look! Peter is perched on that post, shining his light on the doorway so we can see!" She looked up and whispered, "Thank you, Peter."

Joseph tied Fergus near the entrance, and they carefully stepped inside. One of the small pens was empty, filled with soft, fresh straw.

"This will be perfect," Mary said. "Joseph, please go and get some water and clean cloths from the inn. I think ... the baby is coming soon."

As Joseph turned to go, they heard a rustling near the doorway. Peter was sitting on top of the stable door, watching over them.

"Thank you, Peter," Mary said softly. "You helped us find a safe place."

Peter let out a loud *"Wark, wark, wark!"* Then, with a powerful flap of his wings, he soared into the sky and disappeared. Joseph returned quickly with the water and cloths. That night, in the quiet warmth of the stable, baby Jesus was born.

But Peter wasn't gone. He knew the night would get cold, and Mary and Joseph would need more warmth. So he flew out across the town, looking for his friend Excel, the great desert falcon. Peter had one more important mission – to bring help to keep the new-born baby safe and warm.

Dawnlight the Donkey Brings the Firewood

Even though the day had been warm and sunny, the night air began to turn chilly. High above the quiet town of Bethlehem, stars twinkled like little lanterns in the deep purple sky. The hills were hushed, and the only sound was the soft rustle of hay in the nearby stable. At the doorway of that stable stood Dawnlight, a shiny black donkey with gentle brown eyes and long, velvet-soft ears. She stamped her hooves on the ground and shook

her head, her thick coat shivering slightly in the crisp air. Donkeys are tough animals, but even they feel the cold when the frost begins to bite.

Dawnlight looked up at the stars. The sky was so clear she could see every shimmer and sparkle.

"It's going to be a very cold night," she thought. "Too cold for a tiny baby."

She turned her head and peeked inside the stable. Mary was lying quietly on a soft bed of straw, her face calm but tired. Joseph had made her as comfortable as he could after their long journey from Nazareth. Dawnlight had carried Mary all that way, step by careful step, over hills and stony roads. But now something was troubling Dawnlight. She stopped stamping and stood still. Then her ears twitched, and her head shook even harder.

"What if the baby gets cold when he is born?" she worried. "What if Mary doesn't have thick blankets or baby clothes? I remember passing a fire in the courtyard of the inn when we arrived. There was a big pile of logs nearby."

Her eyes lit up.

"That's it! I'll fetch some firewood. Then Joseph can build a fire to keep them warm."

But then she realized something – **she was tied up!**

A thick rope connected her to a wooden post by the stable door. It was too strong to break, and her teeth couldn't chew through it. Just then, she heard Joseph's voice. He was returning from the inn with a bowl of water and clean cloths for Mary.

"If I stand in his way," thought Dawnlight, "he'll have to untie me!"

She tugged at the rope and shuffled across, planting her sturdy body right in front of the door. Her hooves dug into the earth. Moments later, Joseph arrived. He sighed.

"Dawnlight, you silly animal. Move!"

But she didn't move an inch. Joseph pulled at the rope, but Dawnlight stayed firm.

"Fine," he huffed. "You're too stubborn. I'll tie you up at the back of the stable instead."

As soon as he loosened the rope, Dawnlight gave a mighty leap! She twisted, bucked, and dashed off into the night, her hooves thudding softly on the earth. Joseph jumped back in surprise and shouted after her, but Dawnlight didn't look back. She galloped toward the inn's courtyard, where the last glowing fire still flickered, casting dancing shadows on the walls.

Men sat nearby drinking from clay cups, laughing and telling stories. Dawnlight trotted up to the big pile of logs and began stamping her hooves on it.

Thump! Stomp! Thump!

"Oi! What's this donkey doing?" one man grumbled.

"She's after the logs," said another. "Let's give her some before she knocks the whole pile over!"

The men laughed and loaded several logs into the panniers – two baskets strapped to Dawnlight's sides. Satisfied, Dawnlight turned and trotted back into the night. The moon lit her path as she made her way back to the stable. When she arrived, she knocked on the wooden door with her hoof.

Tap-tap-tap.

Inside, Joseph opened the door.

"Dawnlight?" he said in disbelief. "You came back… and you brought firewood? Goodness me!"

He saw the logs in her panniers and quickly carried them inside.

"Thank you, old girl," he whispered. "This will help keep Mary and the baby warm."

In the middle of the stable was a special pit in the ground, made just for safe fires. Joseph stacked some of the logs carefully. But there was one problem… he had no matches. They hadn't been invented yet!

He scratched his head.

"Now… how do I light it?" he murmured. "We'll need a spark… somehow."

But just then, high above the stable, an eagle named Excel was watching. And he had a very bright idea…

Excel the Eagle Brings the Fire

High above the stable, in the tallest cedar tree on the hillside, sat Excel, a grand and noble eagle. His feathers were golden-brown, his beak curved and sharp, and his eyes were as bright as polished glass marbles. From his perch in the topmost branch, Excel could see everything.

He watched the peaceful hills, the glimmering town, and most of all, the small stable below where Mary and Joseph had taken shelter. Excel noticed Joseph step out into the night and walk quietly along the stony path holding an empty bowl. He didn't go into the inn but headed straight for the courtyard, where a few men still sat around a fading fire.

Curious, Excel tilted his head. He saw the men shake their heads and wag their fingers as Joseph spoke. Then, one of the men stood, picked up a glowing branch from the dying fire, and handed it to Joseph. Carefully, Joseph turned and began to walk back toward the stable. But the stable was far – over four hundred metres away. And the night air was cold. As Joseph walked, the glowing stick began to dim. By the time he reached the stable door, it was barely more than a smudge of blackened wood. No glow. No flame. Not even smoke.

Excel's feathers ruffled in concern. He leaned forward on the branch.

Joseph tried again. He turned and hurried back down the path. This time, the men were more helpful. One of them, who looked like a shepherd in his wool cloak and sandals, bent low to the fire. He blew and blew, sending orange sparks flying up into the air like tiny shooting stars. Then, when the flames grew stronger, he carefully passed Joseph a brighter, fierier branch.

Joseph clutched it and walked quickly – but again, the flames died before he reached the stable. Joseph dropped the stick to the ground in frustration.

"It's no use," he muttered. The road was too long. The fire never made it.

Back inside the stable, Mary waited quietly on a bed of straw, her hands resting gently on her belly. Joseph knelt beside her, holding the bowl of water he'd brought. They both looked tired. And cold.

Excel watched it all. His golden eyes blinked slowly.

"I can help," he thought. **"I can fly faster than Joseph can walk."**

He looked once more at the fire in the courtyard. The men had gone now. The inn was quiet, and the fire still glowed gently in the middle of the courtyard. Nobody was watching it. The logs crackled softly. Excel opened his mighty wings. With one strong push, he soared from the treetop, diving like a silent arrow. He landed gracefully on a rock beside the fire and searched for the right branch – one that was still burning at one end, but safe to carry at the other.

He found it.

With care, he took the cool end in his beak. Then, with a powerful leap, he took off into the sky, climbing high and swooping low.

In less than three seconds, Excel reached the stable. He dipped through the open doorway and flew across to the firepit in the centre of the room. That's where Joseph had stacked the wood Dawnlight had brought earlier, and where he had carefully arranged dry grass and twigs. Excel dropped the glowing branch right onto the pile, then turned and soared back to his treetop, his heart beating fast.

At first, all was still.

Then, Joseph rushed forward and picked up the branch. He placed it deep in the middle of the wood and gently blew on it. Sparks danced. The grass crackled. A flame flickered… then caught.

The fire blazed to life.

Warm orange light filled the stable. It danced across the walls and made the straw glow golden. Mary smiled. Joseph let out a deep sigh of relief. The stable was warm at last.

Excel watched from above, proud and content. Thanks to his brave flight, the family would stay cosy through the coldest night. And when baby Jesus arrived, he would be greeted by firelight and warmth – not frost.

Caroline the Chicken's Special Gift

As dawn tiptoed over the hills of Bethlehem, a soft golden light began to peek through the cracks in the wooden stable. The stars were fading, and the world was beginning to stretch and yawn after a long, cold night.

Inside the stable, it was calm and peaceful. A small fire glowed gently in the firepit. The air was warm and filled with the sweet smell of straw and fresh hay. In the manger, wrapped in soft cloths and cradled in a bed of straw, lay baby Jesus. Mary smiled as she watched him sleeping, and Joseph sat close by, gently keeping the fire alive.

But in the far corner of the stable, behind the innkeeper's heavy wine skins and some empty wooden crates, there was a little flurry of movement.

Caroline the chicken was awake.

She was a proud white hen with bright eyes and feathers so clean they shimmered like snow. She ruffled her wings and gave a quiet **"Puck-puck,"** checking to make sure no one had found her secret.

Because behind the crates, hidden in a cosy little nest, lay her treasure – **six warm, speckled eggs**.

Caroline had laid them carefully over the past few days, and she was saving them. She wasn't quite sure what for – but something in her heart told her that soon, she would know.

That morning, as the light spilled across the straw, Caroline watched Mary and the new baby from her hiding place. She had never seen anything like it. The way Mary gently stroked Jesus's tiny hands, the way Joseph tended the fire, the way every animal seemed quieter, softer, more still than usual.

"He really is special," thought Caroline. **"Everyone can feel it."**

Just then, Jesus stirred. His eyes fluttered open, and he let out a tiny cry. Mary lifted him, gently rocking him in her arms. Caroline's feathers tingled. She knew what she had to do.

"The baby will need food," she clucked to herself. **"He will grow strong, and his mother will need something good to eat. It's time."**

She quietly waddled out from behind the crates and used her beak to roll one of the eggs forward.

Then another. And another.

One by one, she gently pushed all six eggs out into the open, right near where Joseph was adding another log to the fire. He turned and spotted them. "Well, what have we here?" he said in surprise. "Caroline, are these from you?"

Caroline gave a proud **"Puck!"** and lifted her head high.

Joseph chuckled.

"Thank you, old girl. These will be perfect."

He gently gathered the eggs into a little basket and brought them to Mary, who smiled gratefully.

"Boiled eggs and warm bread – what a gift," she said.

Caroline clucked happily and returned to her corner. Her nest was empty now, but her heart was full.

She knew she had done something important – **she had shared the best of what she had** for someone very special.

And as the morning sun began to shine brighter, she fluffed her feathers, gave one last proud **"Puck-puck!"** and settled down to rest, ready for whatever the new day might bring.

Mischief the Mouse Celebrates the Birth

It was the very early hours of the morning – those quiet, sleepy moments just before dawn. Outside the stable, all of Bethlehem was resting. The stars were still out, glittering like tiny diamonds on a velvet sky, and even the gentle breeze had gone still.

Inside the cosy stable, everything was silent.

In the very corner of the building, tucked behind a pile of old hay and nestled deep within a tiny hole in the wall, a small grey mouse blinked himself awake. His name was Mischief, and he was as curious as he was cautious.

He twitched his nose and peeped out of his mousehole. His tummy gave a little rumble.

"Maybe now's the right time for a snack," he thought. **"A little bit of supper… or breakfast? I'll call it supp-fast!"**

Mischief's eyes darted around the stable. Was it safe to come out?

Candy the cow stood in her stall, her heavy eyelids drooping. Mischief smiled to himself. He knew there wasn't enough room for her to lie down, so she often slept standing, swaying gently like a tree in the wind.

The chickens were nestled in their straw, their feathers fluffed and beaks tucked under their wings. Another good sign. But Mischief's heart skipped a beat.

"Where is Casper?"

Casper was the stable's watchful cat. With her tortoiseshell coat and clever green eyes, she moved like a whisper and hunted like a shadow. Mischief had lost family members to her stealthy paws – and none of them had ever come back.

He sniffed the air again. No sign of her. Maybe – just maybe – it was safe enough for a little nibble tonight.

He was just about to creep out when – suddenly – **a great cry rang out from the other side of the stable!**

"**Aahhh!**"

Mischief froze, his whiskers standing straight. Then came another, louder voice, bursting with joy:

"It's a boy! Hurrah!"

Mischief's tiny eyes widened.

"Mary's baby!" he whispered. **"He's been born!"**

And then came a soft, loving voice – gentle and full of wonder. It floated through the air like the flutter of an angel's wing:

"His name is Jesus," said Mary. **"I was told before he was born that he must be called Jesus, and that he would be very special."**

The stable, once so quiet, suddenly came alive.

Candy the cow let out a warm, welcoming **"Moo!"**
The sheep stirred in their sleep and answered with a **"Baa!"**
Casper, who had been napping silently on a beam above, let out a surprised **"Meow!"**
Daniel the innkeeper's dog barked softly – **"Ruff-ruff!"** – from his cosy spot near the door.
And from the corner behind the wine skins, Caroline the chicken gave a proud and motherly **"Puck-puck!"**

Every animal seemed to know something special had just happened. The stable was full of joy. Even the spiders in the rafters paused their spinning to listen, and the little owl outside hooted softly into the starry sky.

Mischief's tiny heart was bursting with excitement. He had never seen anything like this before. He was just a mouse – a very small mouse – but tonight, he wanted to be part of the celebration too.

"I can squeak!" he said proudly. **"I may not be big, but I can squeak louder than I ever have before!"**

And he did.

"Squeeeeeak! Squeak! SQUEAK!"

He squeaked so loudly and so joyfully that even the chickens turned their heads.

He squeaked for one minute. Then another. Then another. Three whole minutes of joyful mouse-squeaking filled the stable.

It was the happiest night Mischief had ever known.

He wasn't just a mouse anymore. He was part of something big. Something special. A moment the world would never forget.

And Mischief the Mouse was there – squeaking with joy at the birth of baby Jesus.

Phantom the Fox and Felicity's Gift

Far beyond the warm stable and the glowing firelight, the land stretched out into the cool, quiet night. Silver moonlight painted the desert sands, and every rock cast a long, dark shadow.

In the distance, among the low hills and olive trees, a red fox padded silently over the earth. His name was **Phantom**, and he moved like a ghost – soft and swift, with a coat that shimmered in shades of gold and rust.

Beside him trotted his mate, **Felicity**, a smaller fox with bright eyes and a tail as fluffy as a feather duster. They had been watching from afar, listening to the sounds floating from the stable – a baby's cry, the laughter of animals, and the crackling of a newly lit fire.

Felicity paused and raised her nose to the wind.

"Something wonderful has happened tonight," she said. **"Did you hear the cheers? A child has been born in that little wooden shelter."**

Phantom nodded. His ears twitched.

"I heard," he replied softly. **"The animals were celebrating. Even the chickens and mice."**

Felicity looked up at her mate. **"We must bring them something. A gift. That baby will need food. The mother too."**

Phantom tilted his head. He didn't often share food, but tonight felt different. Very different.

"Then I shall find something," he said. **"Something worthy of such a night."**

With a flick of his tail, Phantom bounded away through the brush. Felicity followed close behind.

Soon they reached the riverbank, where reeds swayed gently in the moonlight. Phantom crouched low and listened. A rustle. A hop. And then – with a flash of movement – he pounced. A moment later, he returned to Felicity, carrying a fine, plump rabbit in his jaws. The perfect gift.

Together, they ran silently back toward the stable.

When they arrived, Phantom crept up to the door, careful not to be seen. He gently placed the rabbit near the firepit just outside, his eyes glowing in the dim light. Then, as quietly as he came, he turned to go.

But the stable door creaked open.

"A fox!" cried Joseph, stepping outside.

Phantom froze for just a second – long enough for their eyes to meet. Then he dashed into the darkness, his paws leaving no sound behind him.

Joseph looked down and saw the rabbit.

"What on Earth?" he whispered. **"A fox… bringing a gift?"**

He knelt beside the rabbit and touched its soft fur.

"We have food," he said, amazed. **"Enough for days."**

Back on the hill, Phantom and Felicity sat beneath an olive tree, watching the warm light flicker from the stable. Felicity nudged Phantom's shoulder.

"You were very brave."

Phantom gave a small, proud nod.

"We may not stay close to others," he said, **"but tonight, we helped in the only way we could."**

And so the two foxes curled up beneath the stars, tails wrapped around their noses, hearts full. For even the wildest of creatures had a place in this magical night. Even a fox – silent and swift – could bring warmth and kindness to the manger of a king.

Bluey the Blackbird Mends the Roof

It was still early morning, and soft grey clouds hung low in the sky above Bethlehem. Most of the village was still asleep, but a light rain had begun to fall. Gentle at first, then a little harder.

Inside the warm stable, Mary and Joseph sat close to the firepit, watching over their new-born baby, Jesus. He lay peacefully in the manger, wrapped in soft cloths and bits of wool, gently sleeping as the rain pattered above.

Suddenly, Joseph looked up.

"Gosh," he said, turning to Mary. **"It doesn't rain often in Bethlehem, but it's really coming down now – and there's a leak in the roof!"**

He pointed to a patch right above the manger, where droplets of water were beginning to fall.

"If this gets worse, we'll have to move him. We can't let him get wet."

Up under the eaves of the stable, tucked into a nest made of twigs and straw, sat a little blackbird named **Bluey**. She had been watching everything from her perch for the last day. Bluey had built the nest with her mate, **Blackie**, and they had been planning to raise a family there.

Though most blackbirds are completely black, Bluey had a single bright blue feather in her tail – so bright and shiny that her mother, Black-as-Night, had named her after it.

Bluey had listened closely to all the excitement below. She and Blackie had chirped with joy when the baby had been born. And they'd even overheard that their distant cousin, Caroline the Chicken (although neither of them really believed they were related), had given the family eggs for breakfast.

Now, with the rain beginning to fall and the roof beginning to leak, Bluey looked down with worry.

"Oh no," she chirped. **"The baby could get soaked. He's so tiny… he might catch a chill!"**

She looked around. Blackie had flown off earlier to find their supper. She hoped he would return soon – she needed help. Just then, a black blur darted through the air and landed beside her.

"Blackie!" she chirped with relief.

"You won't believe it," she told him. **"The roof is leaking – right over the baby's bed! We must fix it. Could you please go down to the river and bring back some reeds? We could weave them into the hole and stop the rain from coming in."**

But Blackie shook his head.

"Not me," he said, flopping into the nest. **"I've been flying for twenty minutes looking for grubs and worms and couldn't find a thing. I'm exhausted. But you've been sitting here all day. You go, Bluey – you're strong and quick. I'll help you weave the reeds when you get back."**

Bluey opened her beak to protest, but then closed it. She looked once more at the baby below, then nodded firmly.

"Alright," she said. **"For the baby."**

She stretched her wings and launched into the rainy sky. Down she swooped toward the riverbed just outside the village. Flying low, she darted along the bank until she spotted a patch of tall, green bullrushes swaying gently by the slow-moving water.

Using her sharp beak, she pulled at the reeds, one after another, until she had a beak full of long, bendy stems. Then she turned and sped back toward the stable, the reeds trailing behind her like ribbons in the wind.

When she arrived, Blackie was waiting on a post beside the stable door.

"Look!" she chirped through her full beak. **"I brought plenty! Let's fix the roof!"**

Together they flew up to the leaky spot. Blackie held the reeds in place while Bluey carefully tucked and twisted them into the broken gap, weaving them like a basket. They worked quickly, and within five minutes, the hole was sealed tight.

Bluey looked down proudly. Not a single drop of water was falling inside anymore.

"There," she said. **"The baby will stay dry now."**

But Blackie fluffed his feathers.

"While you were gone," he said, **"I checked the rest of the roof… and I found three more cracks where rain might come through!"**

Bluey let out a tiny sigh – but she smiled too.

"Alright," she said. **"I'll go back. Let's make sure the whole roof is safe."**

Down she flew once more, her wings slicing through the air. She returned a few minutes later with another bundle of reeds, and together, she and Blackie sealed every hole they could find. When they were finished, the roof was strong and snug, with not a single drip of rain inside.

The fire still crackled. The baby still slept peacefully. And above, in their cosy little nest under the eaves, Bluey and Blackie cuddled close, proud of what they had done.

"We're not just birds," Bluey whispered, closing her eyes. **"Tonight, we're helpers."**

Spinner the Spider Spins to Protect

In the furthest corner of the stable, where the wooden beams stretched high into the rafters and the shadows were thick and cool, lived a spider named **Spinner**. He had made his home behind one of the posts that helped hold up the stable's roof. Spinner had lived there for almost a whole year, and he knew every nook and cranny of the stable better than anyone.

Spinner wasn't just any spider – he was a true web-weaving champion. From the very tips of his eight legs, he could spin threads of the finest silk, shiny and strong. His legs stretched out nearly 4 centimetres across, and he carried himself with the quiet pride of someone who knew his craft.

Every month, spiders from all across Bethlehem gathered for the great **Spider Web Spinning Competition**. Spinner had always done well – but two months ago, he had come in second place. His web had been described as "nearly perfect" by **Spinnerette**, the wisest and kindest judge. And just last month – he had finally **won**!

Now Spinner was the reigning champion.

He had been quietly watching everything that had happened in the stable over the past day. He'd seen Mary and Joseph arrive, and he had heard the joyful shouts when the baby, Jesus, was born. But Spinner had also seen something that made him rather grumpy.

"That fire is far too big," he muttered from his beam. **"Joseph must've used every log in Bethlehem!"**

The heat from the fire had nearly scorched Spinner's silk threads, and worse – it had started attracting buzzing, flapping, flying insects. Dozens of flies had swarmed inside, drawn to the warmth and the light. They zipped and darted through the air, landing on the cow's nose, buzzing around the donkey's ears, and bothering everyone who was trying to rest.

"If they bite the baby," Spinner whispered, **"he might get sick. We can't have that. No, we most certainly cannot."**

He peered down from his post and spotted a low wooden beam covered in hay – just above the manger where baby Jesus was resting.

"Perfect," he said.

Without another thought, Spinner spun a fresh thread using his back legs. He swung like a tiny acrobat through the air, landing gently on the hay bower. There, he quickly attached another strand and began his work.

Back and forth. Loop by loop. Thread by thread.

In just ten minutes, Spinner had created one of the most beautiful and intricate webs he had ever spun. It shimmered ever so slightly in the soft firelight, like a silver net woven from moonlight itself.

He stood back proudly, perched on one leg, his other seven twitching with satisfaction.

"If I made this for the next competition," he said to himself, **"I might win again. Maybe even earn a piece of that glittering silk from the mountain caves. Oh, how Spidroxia would sulk if I won twice in a row!"**

But Spinner didn't make this web for a prize. He made it for something far more important. Already, he could see the difference. A fly zipped toward the baby – but got caught in the sticky web before it could come close. Another followed – and it too was trapped.

One by one, the pests that could sting or bite were stopped, tangled safely in Spinner's strong, glistening threads.

Below, the baby slept on, peaceful and undisturbed.

Spinner stayed at his post for the rest of the night, guarding the web, watching over the child. No one noticed him. No one clapped or cheered. But Spinner didn't mind. Because sometimes, the smallest of creatures can do the biggest of jobs. And Spinner the Spider had done his – spinning not just a web, but a shield of safety for the baby in the straw.

Barry the Bat Clears the Air

As the sun dipped low behind the hills of Bethlehem and the sky turned dusky purple, the quiet stable grew cooler. A soft breeze whispered through the cracks in the wooden walls, and the fire in the middle flickered gently.

Hanging upside down from the wooden rafters, tucked into a shadowy beam above the manger, was **Barry the bat**. His little claws gripped the wood tightly as he slept, his long ears drooping and his wings wrapped around his furry body like a blanket.

Barry was no ordinary bat – he was a long-eared bat, fast and clever, and he knew every safe hiding place for miles around. Sometimes he napped in the deep caves carved into the cliffs outside town, where old robbers had once hidden from the law. Other times he flew across the desert skies to the rocky edges of the Red Sea, where secret hollows between boulders made cosy, hidden homes.

But of all the places Barry could go, his favourite was the stable.

"It's warm, it's quiet, and it always smells of hay," he would say. **"Perfect for a proper bat nap."**

Tonight, as the light faded and Barry blinked awake, he stretched his wings and looked around. Below him, he noticed Spinner the spider busily weaving a brand-new web above the manger. Barry watched with mild curiosity, twitching one ear.

"That spider again," he muttered. **"Always spinning. Doesn't even look like he's caught anything yet."**

He huffed, flapping his wings gently as he stayed upside down. Spinner's silk threads shimmered in the firelight, but they were still untouched by any fly.

Then Barry froze.

A **large green fly**, with shiny wings and big bulging eyes, zipped down from the rafters. It buzzed through the air and – **oh no!** – landed right on the baby's forehead. Barry held his breath.

Thankfully, Joseph had seen it too. In one swift motion, he waved his hand and brushed the fly away before it could sting or bite. But Barry was alarmed.

"That could have been dangerous!" he said to himself. **"What if next time, someone doesn't see the fly in time?"**

He unhooked his claws, stretched his wings, and dropped silently into the air.

Now it was Barry's turn to help.

He zipped across the stable, flitting this way and that – **so fast, he was just a blur**. He used his special gift – **sonar**, the way bats sense their surroundings with sound – to find and chase every buzzing, biting insect that had crept inside. He twisted, swooped, and looped through the air with incredible speed and grace. Flies barely had a chance to blink before Barry caught them.

Joseph looked up in amazement.

"Just look at that bat!" he said to Mary. **"He's flying so fast – I can't believe he's not bumping into the walls. He must be catching every last fly!"**

And indeed he was. In just a few minutes, the stable air was completely clear. Not a single buzz could be heard.

The animals sighed with relief. Candy the cow rested her head. Surfinia the sheep blinked drowsily. Even Spinner gave a nod of approval from his web. Barry made one final sweep of the stable, then glided back up to his perch. With a flutter, he hooked his claws once more into the beam and tucked himself upside down. His wings wrapped around him like a cape.

Job done.

He had made sure the air around baby Jesus was clear and safe. No stings, no bites – **only peace**.

And as Barry settled back into his favourite spot, the stable quieted once more. The fire crackled, the baby slept soundly, and all the animals knew – **they had each played a part in keeping him safe that night**.

Daniel the Canaan Dog Stands Guard

Daniel was a handsome dog, with a sandy-coloured coat, alert eyes, and a tail that curled just slightly at the tip. He lived at the inn with the innkeeper and his family, and he was no ordinary mutt – Daniel was a proud **Canaan dog**, a very special breed known for being clever, brave, and watchful.

He had lived at the inn for four years and was rather well-known among the travellers who came and went. If anyone dropped a crumb or left their dinner unattended, Daniel would be there in a flash, gently "helping" to clean it up. His favourite treats came from **Sandina**, the innkeeper's wife, who often saved him bits of roast chicken or fish stew from her kitchen.

Daniel also had a great love for creamy milk. Whenever he had the chance, he would sneak into the stable to see if **Candy the Cow** had left behind a wooden bucket with a little milk still sloshing at the bottom. The buckets were not just ordinary buckets – they were hand-carved by the innkeeper himself, made from fallen cedar trees. And after the buckets were made, the innkeeper's daughter, **Claudia**, would paint them with swirls and patterns inspired by the river near their home.

But on this particular morning, Daniel wasn't thinking about milk – or even chicken. He had been awake most of the night, stirred by the strange sounds coming from the

stable: hushed voices, a woman crying out, the crackling of a fire, and then finally... the tiny wail of a new-born.

"A baby," Daniel thought. **"There's a new baby in the stable!"**

As dawn began to brighten the sky, Daniel decided to go and have a look for himself. He padded across the courtyard, his paws silent on the stone, and found that the stable door had been left open just a crack.

Slipping quietly inside, Daniel stopped and looked around. The stable was warm, filled with the soft scent of straw and the gentle glow of a dying fire. Mary and Joseph were fast asleep, curled up beside the fire after a long and tiring night. And resting snugly in a manger, wrapped in soft cloth and wool, was a baby – tiny, perfect, and peacefully awake.

The baby looked up at Daniel and gave a small, happy gurgle.

Daniel's ears perked. But then something else caught his nose. Over by the fire were **three large brown eggs** and a **fresh rabbit**, neatly laid out – waiting, perhaps, to be made into a hot breakfast. Daniel's mouth watered. His stomach gave a quiet growl.

"What a breakfast that would be," he thought. **"Eggs and rabbit! I could carry them back to the inn and have a feast."**

He crept closer… but then stopped. He looked at Mary. He looked at Joseph. And he looked again at the tiny baby, who now had a hand tucked up near his cheek, still making those soft, sweet gurgles.

Daniel sighed.

"No," he thought. **"This food isn't for me. Mary and Joseph have had a long night. They'll be hungry when they wake. And the baby… he may not eat rabbit, but his parents will need their strength to care for him."**

He also thought of **Rankin the Rat**, who had a habit of sneaking into the stable when no one was looking.

"Better I stay and guard the food," Daniel decided. **"Just in case."**

And so he did. Daniel lay down beside the rabbit and the eggs, curling his tail around his legs. He didn't touch a single thing. He just waited, eyes alert, ears twitching at every sound.

Two whole hours passed.

When Joseph finally stirred, blinking and rubbing his eyes, he sat up and stretched. Then he saw Daniel.

"Hey!" he barked. **"What's that dog doing here? Is he trying to eat our breakfast?"**

Joseph grabbed his long walking stick and leapt to his feet. But Daniel was quick. He sprang up, spun around, and darted through the doorway before the stick could even touch the ground. He didn't bark or growl – he simply ran back to the inn, slipped inside, and jumped straight into his basket.

He curled up, yawned once, and within seconds… was fast asleep. He may not have been thanked, but **Daniel the Canaan Dog had done his job**. He had kept watch. He had protected the food. And he had made sure that Mary and Joseph – and especially baby Jesus – would wake to a warm meal after a long night.

Because sometimes the quietest kind of help is also the kindest.

Casper the Cat Stands Watch

In the rafters of the stable, hidden in the shadows near a wide wooden beam, lay **Casper**, the tortoiseshell cat.

His fur was a stunning patchwork of creamy white, fiery red, golden brown, and hints of ginger, especially around his eyes. He was a beautiful cat – and he knew it. So did **Matthias**, the innkeeper who had taken Casper in when he was just a tiny kitten.

But Matthias hadn't taken Casper in just because he was pretty. **Casper had a job**. The inn was a busy place, filled with travellers who dropped crumbs, spilled flour, and sometimes left doors open. And that meant one thing: **rats**.

Matthias needed someone clever and quiet, someone who could keep the inn – and the yard outside – safe from hungry creatures looking for a free meal. Casper had become that someone. He had learned quickly how to sneak and pounce, especially by hiding behind the big sack of flour stored near the back of the barn. After Casper had proved himself as a skilled hunter, Matthias rewarded him with his own bed in the barn – and plenty of food in his supper bowl each night.

"It's your barn now, Casper," Matthias had said. **"Keep it safe."**

And Casper did. For two years, he watched over every corner, every shadow. **No rat dared step inside without thinking twice.**

But this night had been different. Casper had watched, wide-eyed from his beam, as two strangers – Mary and Joseph – were given permission to sleep in the stable. He had never seen the innkeeper allow that before. Then, in the darkest part of the night, the silence had been broken by the soft cries of a new-born baby.

A baby – born right here in his barn.

Casper wasn't sure what to make of it at first. He wasn't usually fond of loud noises or new visitors. But there was something different about this baby. Something gentle. Something peaceful.

Then something moved. From his perch above, Casper saw a flash of grey squeeze under the stable door. It was a **rat** – a large one with a red nose.

"Rednose," Casper hissed under his breath. **"Not you again."**

Rednose lived beneath the wall of the inn with his brothers – **Rampant** and **Rushalong**. They were always sniffing around for food. Casper had chased them many times, but Rednose was fast, and always managed to slip away. Now Rednose scurried across the straw-covered floor, heading for a crust of bread that Joseph had dropped before falling asleep.

But then… Rednose stopped. He sniffed the air. He turned his head.

He had seen the baby. And now he was heading toward the manger.

Casper's fur bristled. His tail twitched. He leapt from the beam like a streak of fire and landed silently on the ground. In one breath, he dashed across the stable, charging straight toward the rat. Rednose squeaked in fright and disappeared back under the door in a flash.

Casper stood tall, his heart thumping.

"That was too close," he thought. **"He might come back. And he might bring his brothers."**

Casper didn't hesitate. He padded softly over to the manger and curled up just beside it. His golden eyes glowed in the low firelight. His ears flicked at every sound. His tail wrapped tightly around his paws.

He would not sleep tonight.

"If I stay right here," he thought, **"no rat or snake or sneaky thief will dare come close."**

And so he stayed. For hours and hours, through the quiet of dawn and into the golden light of morning, **Casper stood guard**. He didn't chase butterflies. He didn't nap. He didn't even go looking for milk or scraps.

He simply watched – silent, still, and strong. He watched until the day Mary and Joseph gently lifted their baby and set off on their journey. Only then did Casper stretch, blink his sleepy eyes, and return to his place on the beam.

He was proud. Because even though he was just a cat, **he had helped keep the most special baby in the world safe through the night**.

Candy the Cow Shares Her Milk

Inside the stable, in the cosiest corner near a wall of stacked hay, stood a beautiful brown and white cow named **Candy**.

Candy was a proud **Holstein cow**, and she looked every bit the part. Her fur was soft and smooth, with elegant white legs and patches of creamy brown across her back and belly. She had gentle eyes, a long tail that swished when she was thinking, and a big heart full of kindness.

Just ten weeks earlier, Candy had given birth to her first **calf** – or rather, to her great surprise **two calves**! A boy and a girl – **Candid** and **Candida**.

The innkeeper had been so delighted about the twins that he'd decided Candy and her little ones should sleep inside the stable each night, where it was warm and safe. Candy loved her calves with all her heart. Every morning and evening, she fed them herself, giving them fresh, creamy milk – just as nature intended. They drank as much as they could, their little tails wagging happily, and they were growing fast and strong.

But Candy wasn't just any cow. She was a thoughtful cow. And over the past day, she had quietly watched from her stall as something truly special happened in the stable. She had seen Mary and Joseph arrive, tired from their journey. She had watched as

Mary gave birth to a tiny baby boy. And she had listened with awe as the other animals whispered to one another,

"His name is Jesus."

Candy had also watched as Mary lovingly fed her baby with her own milk.

"How clever humans are," thought Candy. **"Just like cows. They feed their babies with love, just like I feed Candid and Candida."**

But early the next morning, something made Candy's ears prick up. She heard Joseph speaking softly to Mary.

"You seem to be running low on milk," he said gently. **"I'll go and ask the innkeeper if he can spare some for the baby."**

Candy's heart thudded.

"Oh no," she thought. **"The baby needs milk and may not have enough!"**

A few minutes later, Joseph returned – with the innkeeper by his side.

"We've only just enough milk for the breakfast guests," the innkeeper explained. **"But if Mary can't feed the baby, that changes everything. Candy may be able to help."**

Candy blinked. She was listening very closely now. The innkeeper pulled up a little wooden stool beside her and took a beautifully carved wooden bucket from under his apron. He had made it himself, just like all the buckets in the inn. His daughter, Claudia, had even painted waves and stones along the side of it to make it look like the river nearby.

Candy snorted in surprise. She hadn't expected to be milked this early. Her tail twitched, and she even thought for a moment about kicking over the bucket.

"My milk is for my babies!" she thought angrily.

But then she looked across the stable at the sleeping child in the manger. His tiny hands were curled gently under his chin. His breath rose and fell softly. And suddenly, Candy knew what she had to do.

"That baby needs milk," she thought. **"More than anyone."**

She stood still. She didn't kick. She didn't twitch. She let the innkeeper fill the bucket with her best, creamiest milk.

"I can eat more hay," she told herself. **"I'll make more milk later for Candid and Candida. They'll be just fine."**

The innkeeper milked her for ten whole minutes, gently and carefully. When the bucket was nearly full, he stood up and gave Candy a pat on the side.

"Well done, Candy," he said with a grin. **"This is wonderful milk. And as a thank you, you'll get an extra stook of fresh hay for breakfast."**

Candy blinked in surprise. The innkeeper had never praised her like that before!

"If all it takes is a little milk to help," she thought happily, **"then I'll give a little more every day while the baby stays with us."**

And with a soft **moo**, Candy turned to check on her calves – who were still fast asleep – and settled herself down for a bit of rest, her heart full of warmth. Because even though she was just a cow, Candy had done something big.

She had shared her gift of milk with baby Jesus.

Surfinia the Sheep Gives Her Wool

Late in the night, long after the stars had come out, the innkeeper stood outside the front door of the inn, gazing up at the sky. The stars sparkled more brightly than he had ever seen before, and the cool air brushed his cheeks.

"Look at that sky," he said to his wife, who stood beside him. **"The stars are dancing! It's beautiful – but it's going to be a very cold night. There'll be frost by morning, I'm sure of it. I'll need to light a fire early to thaw out the milk and water for our guests."**

He paused for a moment, then added,

"Before we go to bed, I'd better check on that couple in the stable – Mary and Joseph. They have a new-born baby. I must make sure they know to keep him wrapped up warmly."

He pulled on his warmest sheepskin jacket and headed to the stable, his footsteps crunching on the frozen ground. Inside the stable, Mary and Joseph had done all they could. Their baby, Jesus, was wrapped in cloths and gently placed in a manger filled with straw. Mary was curled beside him, trying to keep warm, while Joseph tended the fire.

But by three o'clock in the morning, the temperature had fallen to **-5°C**. A hard frost crept across the fields, and even inside the stable, the cold bit at every corner. Suddenly, baby Jesus began to cry – loud and strong.

Mary sat up, worry filling her eyes.

"Joseph," she said, her voice trembling, **"He's shivering. He's freezing. If we can't warm him soon, he might get very sick… or worse. Please, Joseph. I've done all I can. I've fed him, I've wrapped him – but now you must help. We need something more."**

Joseph felt helpless. He looked around, wishing for another blanket or thicker clothes, but there was nothing more to give. Just a few feet away, standing quietly in her stall, was **Surfinia**, a gentle sheep with a thick, snowy-white coat.

Surfinia had seen everything. She had watched the birth of baby Jesus the night before, and she had felt the joy and wonder that had filled the stable. Now, hearing his cries, she felt fear too.

"He's so small," she thought. **"He mustn't be left in the cold."**

Then, an idea warmed her heart.

"I can help," she whispered to herself. **"I have wool – so much wool! I can give it to him."**

She lifted her head and called out in her loudest voice:

"Baa! Baa! Humaldson! Harriet! Come down quickly!"

High above in the rafters, two sleepy house sparrows blinked awake in their little nest. **Humaldson** and **Harriet** fluttered their wings and zipped down to Surfinia's side.

"What is it?" chirped Harriet. **"Is something wrong?"**

"The baby," said Surfinia, her voice filled with worry. **"He's freezing. His parents are desperate. I want you to pull tufts of wool from my coat and carry them to him. My wool is the warmest in all of Bethlehem. It might be the only thing that can help."**

Without another word, the two birds got to work. Surfinia lay down, raising her thick coat to make it easier. The sparrows gently tugged mouthfuls of soft wool, their beaks full, and flew across the stable to drop the wool near Joseph.

Again and again they flew, gathering more wool, until a soft pile formed beside the fire. Joseph looked up, bewildered.

"Where is this wool coming from?" he said. **"It's falling from the sky!"**

Mary didn't care where it came from. She grabbed the wool, rolled it into long strands, and quickly wove them into a little coat with sleeves – just the right size for a new-born. She wrapped Jesus snugly in the wool, pulled him close, and smiled.

Almost immediately, the baby stopped crying. His breathing slowed. His face relaxed.

"He's warm again," Mary said gently. **"He's going to be fine."**

She kissed his forehead and placed him gently back in the manger.

"I don't know where that wool came from," she whispered, **"but it saved him."**

Up in her stall, Surfinia smiled and rested her head. Beside her, Humaldson and Harriet nestled back into their nest, feathers fluffed with pride. They had done something truly special. And no one – **not even a little sheep or two tiny sparrows** – was too small to make a big difference.

Madge the Magpie Pays the Bill

Three days and three nights had passed since Mary and Joseph arrived in Bethlehem. The little stable behind the inn had become their home, and it was where their baby – **Jesus** – had been born under the glow of the stars and the kindness of strangers.

During those days, the innkeeper and his wife had been very kind. Each morning, they brought creamy milk for the baby, soft bread, and tasty cheese for Mary and Joseph. Once or twice, they'd even sent sweet oranges – and juicy figs too (though Mary was allergic, so Joseph ate them all and said they were delicious!).

But now, it was time to leave. Joseph packed their few belongings and helped Mary get ready for the journey home. As he fastened the bundles to their donkey's back, his face grew troubled. He sat down on a wooden box, opened his small leather purse, and sighed.

"Mary," he said softly, **"we only have 150 denarii left. I don't know if it will be enough to pay the innkeeper. Yes, we stayed in his stable... but he's given us so much food, and I may have... well... enjoyed more than a few flagons of his wine."**

Mary smiled gently but said nothing. She trusted Joseph – and trusted that somehow, things would be alright.

High above them in the rafters of the stable, perched on a wide wooden beam, sat a sharp-eyed magpie named **Madge**. She had been living in the rafters for many months. Her feathers were shiny black and white, with bright white patches along her chest and wingtips that glistened when the moonlight touched them.

Madge had watched everything that had happened in the stable – from tired travellers' arrival to the birth of the baby, and the kindness that filled the barn since that night. Now, hearing Joseph's worried voice, she tilted her head.

"Can't pay the bill?" Madge whispered to herself. **"Well, I know what to do. I see shiny coins lying about in the streets all the time. I can find enough to help!"**

With that, she spread her wings and swooped silently out of the stable and into the golden morning light. Madge darted through the alleys and side streets of Bethlehem, soaring past shop stalls and rooftops, narrowly missing the tall chimney of the Roman town hall. She knew the town well – she knew where the sun hit just right and made shiny things sparkle.

Near the riverbank, something caught her eye. A glint of silver. Lying right on the sand.

She dived fast – faster than she had ever flown before – and snatched the coin up in her beak. It was a **20-denarii piece**, shiny and warm from the sun. With a whoosh, she was back at the stable, circling in from above. She dropped the coin right at **Joseph's feet**, then fluttered back to the rafters.

Joseph blinked in surprise.

"What on Earth…?" he said, reaching down. **"A coin? Where did this come from?"** He looked up and noticed a flash of feathers disappearing into the shadows.

"Could it have been that magpie? No… surely not."

But over the next hour, Madge returned **again and again**, bringing coin after coin. One she found near the blacksmith's shop, another beside the well, and even one in the dust outside the temple gates. Each time, she dropped her shiny treasure beside Joseph without a sound.

After her **fifth trip**, Joseph counted the coins – and then counted again.

"I can't believe it!" he exclaimed. **"We have almost 300 denarii now. Enough to pay the innkeeper – and still have some left for the journey home."**

He looked up to the rafters, and there she was – Madge, sitting tall and proud on her favourite beam, watching him closely.

Joseph grinned. And then, with a chuckle, he **winked**.

To his amazement… **Madge winked back**.

He laughed aloud.

"I didn't know birds could wink," he said. **"But I suppose this one can."**

As they prepared to leave the stable later that day, Joseph gave the innkeeper the full payment – and a little extra. The innkeeper was surprised.

"Where did you find all this?" he asked.

Joseph just smiled.

"Let's just say… we had help from above."

And high in the rafters, **Madge the Magpie** tucked her beak under her wing, and finally took a well-earned nap – her job done, her heart full.

Antwerp the Ass Announces the Birth

Antwerp the donkey stood quietly in his stall, watching. He hadn't slept much – not for two whole nights. Not because he was uncomfortable, but because something very special had happened in his stable, and he hadn't wanted to miss a moment.

He had seen it all: the arrival of Mary and Joseph, the birth of the baby Jesus, and all the small, thoughtful acts of kindness from his fellow animals. He had seen **Excel the Eagle** soar through the air with a burning branch to light the fire.

He had watched **Caroline the Chicken** give her eggs, and **Surfinia the sheep** offer her warm wool.

He had heard **Madge the Magpie** drop coin after coin beside Joseph. Even the tiniest creatures – like **Mischief the Mouse** and **Spinner the Spider** – had done their part.

Everyone had found a way to help. But Antwerp? He felt a little lost.

"What can I do?" he wondered, his ears drooping. **"I don't have eggs or wool or wings. I don't even know how to catch flies like Barry the bat. I want to give something too... but I don't have anything to offer."**

He sighed, standing still in the straw.

What he didn't realise was that high above him, **Excelsior the Eagle**, brother to Excel, had quietly landed on Antwerp's broad back. He had noticed some small insects hiding in the donkey's thick coat and had begun to nibble them up – after all, eagles found such things quite tasty!

But Excelsior got a little too excited. He pecked – **hard**.

"YEEE-OWWW!" Antwerp cried, rearing back his head and letting out the loudest, longest **bray** the stable had ever heard. Excelsior flapped up in surprise and disappeared into the rafters.

Antwerp blinked… then paused.

"Wait a minute," he said to himself slowly. **"That's it. That's what I can do!"**

He stood tall, his hooves steady beneath him.

"I can bray. Not just any bray – I can bray louder than any other donkey in all of Bethlehem. Maybe even the world!"

His eyes sparkled as he looked over to the sleeping baby in the manger.

"Everyone says this baby is special. That he'll grow up to change everything. That he'll bring peace and fairness to the world – not just for people, but for every creature that walks, flies, swims, or crawls. Even donkeys."

And with that, **Antwerp opened his mouth** and let out a mighty, joyful bray:

"HEE-HAWWWWWWW!"

He didn't stop. He brayed through the morning, through the afternoon, and even into the night. For **thirty hours**, Antwerp the donkey brayed his heart out. If you happened to understand **donkey language**, you would've heard something like this:

"A baby has been born in Bethlehem! He has come to bring peace, fairness, and joy to the whole world – so that every human can live with kindness in their hearts, and every animal can live in harmony too!"

"Let the world know: something wonderful has happened!"

From the distant hills, shepherds looked up. In nearby fields, animals pricked up their ears.

Even some sleepy villagers stirred in their beds, hearing the message in the wind.

Antwerp didn't stop until every corner of Bethlehem had heard his voice. And when at last he lay down to rest, tired but proud, he knew deep in his heart that he had given his gift too – his voice.

And it had **carried the message of hope across the land**.

Daisychain the Duck Makes a Toy

On a quiet little pond, just to the right of the inn in Bethlehem, there lived a beautiful eider duck named **Daisychain**. Her feathers were soft and snowy white, her beak as orange as a ripe apricot, and her eyes sparkled with kindness. She was almost two years old and had lived at this peaceful pond ever since she was a duckling.

Daisychain had once lived with her mother, **Daisy**, and her father, **Diamond**, on another pond just a few miles away. She had three siblings – **Derek, Dancer, and Darkbill** – but sadly, she had been the only one to grow up.

When she was six months old, her father had gently told her it was time to leave home and find her own pond. That was how Daisychain had come to the little pool near the Bethlehem inn, where the reeds swayed softly and the sky was always wide and open.

Not long after, a familiar shape appeared in the sky – it was **Diamond**, circling down with a flutter of wings. To Daisychain's joy, he had found her again, and together they had built a cosy nest among the rushes at the pond's edge. But just a week ago, Diamond had flown off to explore a new home, promising to return soon. Daisychain had waited patiently, her eyes always scanning the horizon.

That was how she happened to be watching when Mary and Joseph came down the dusty path and entered the stable at the inn. Soon after, she learned from the other animals that a **baby** had been born – **a very special baby** named **Jesus**.

Daisychain waddled back to the water's edge and stared at the moonlit ripples.

"Everyone has given the baby something," she thought. **"But what can I give?"**

She looked down at her chest, where her softest feathers were tucked. Then she remembered something her mother had once told her:

"When I laid your egg, I placed it in the warmest part of the nest and covered it with my duck down. Duck down is one of the warmest and softest things in the world."

"That's it!" Daisychain quacked. **"I'll make a soft ball of duck down for baby Jesus to play with – and to help keep him warm."**

She carefully plucked tiny tufts of down from her breast – soft, white, and light as feathers on the wind. She shaped them into a little ball, rolling it gently in her beak until it was smooth and fluffy.

Just as she was about to take off toward the stable, she heard a *whoosh* in the sky – and with a splash and a flurry of feathers, **Diamond** landed beside her.

"Diamond! You're back!" she cried. **"Quick! I need your help. I'm making a gift for the baby in the stable. A toy made of duck down to keep him warm. Can you spare some of yours?"**

"Of course!" said Diamond proudly. **"Let's make it the best duck down ball in all of Bethlehem."**

Together, they added more of Diamond's soft feathers until the little ball was double in size – fluffier, warmer, and more perfect than ever. With the gift tucked safely in her beak, **Daisychain lifted off into the moonlit sky**, her wings strong and steady. She soared over the pond, past the sleeping inn, and through the open doorway of the stable.

Inside, the fire flickered low, and Mary was gently rocking her baby in her arms.

Daisychain hovered near the manger and dropped the duck down ball just a few feet from the crib. Then, with a flap of her wings, she slipped out again into the night. Back at the pond, Diamond was waiting.

"Did you find the crib?" he asked.

"I did," said Daisychain. **"And I left our gift right beside it."**

She smiled as she settled into the nest beside him. And inside the stable, when Joseph picked up the small ball of down and placed it gently beside the sleeping child, Mary smiled.

"What a soft toy," she whispered. **"So light, and warm, and comforting. Wherever it came from… it was made with love."**

The Visit of the Shepherds

Far away from the inn, up on the rugged hills beyond the edge of Bethlehem, **three shepherds** sat by their fire, finishing bowls of hot milk as the stars blinked above them. Their names were **Jaspar**, **Jonzamil**, and **Janzid** – three friends who had watched over their flock through many a night.

Jaspar was especially tired. Earlier that day, **three tiny lambs** – only two days old – had escaped from the korale, the safe stone pen where new lambs were kept. Jaspar had chased them for hours up the rocky hilltops and, thankfully, brought them back safely.

Jonzamil was worn out too. After the lambs had been found, Janzid had ordered him to carry large stones up from the valley to strengthen the walls of the korale. It was hard work, but Janzid was not someone you argued with – he had once been a fierce warrior, and everyone respected his command.

As for **Janzid**, he was having a good day. The lambs were safe, the pen was secure, and he had spent the afternoon doing something he loved – **knitting**. His camel hair and lamb's wool shirt was nearly finished, and he hoped to wear it at the next holy feast.

Just as their fire began to dim, **a brilliant flash** lit up the sky. The three men jumped to their feet.

"Look up there!" cried Jaspar, pointing. **"That star – it's never been there before!"**

It glowed brighter than any other star in the sky. It shimmered and danced, as if singing a song made of light.

"It must be a sign," said Jonzamil softly. **"A new star… it must mean something has happened. Or is about to happen."**

Before they could speak further, **three camels** emerged from the shadows, their hooves kicking up dust as they walked. On each camel sat a rider, dressed in fine robes and shimmering turbans.

"Greetings," said the first rider. **"We've been following that star for days. Our wise man says a new king has been born nearby. We're heading to Jerusalem to ask King Herod about it. Is this the way?"**

The shepherds pointed them in the right direction, and the riders thanked them and disappeared into the night.

The hilltop was quiet again. Janzid broke the silence.

"When I went down to Bethlehem this morning to buy flour, the whole village was buzzing. People were talking about a baby born in the stable behind the inn. The rooms were full, so the innkeeper gave the family a place with the animals."

The Visit of the Shepherds

"That must be him," said Jonzamil. **"The king the star is announcing!"**

"Then we should go and see him," said Jaspar. **"We may be simple shepherds, but it feels like we're meant to meet this baby."**

"Let's bring a gift," said Janzid. **"We don't have gold or treasures, but what about a lamb? A gift for the child to grow up with."**

The three shepherds chose the **purest lamb** they had – an albino one with a snow-white coat and pink-tinted ears. It was rare and special, the most beautiful lamb in their flock.

"Let this be our gift," said Jaspar. **"He can keep it as his own, and when he grows older, he'll know that we came to honour him."**

Before they left, they made sure the korale was tightly sealed – **no more runaway lambs tonight**. Then, wrapped in their sheepskin cloaks and guiding the lamb gently by a rope, the shepherds set off down the hillside, following the light of the star.

An hour later, they stood inside the warm stable. They knelt by the manger and looked down at the sleeping baby.

"We have brought him a lamb," said Jaspar softly.

Joseph looked at them kindly. **"That's very generous. But we have no land or pasture in Nazareth. We cannot take the lamb with us. Please – return it to its**

mother. Let it live and grow with the flock. That will bring joy to her… and to the lamb."

The shepherds nodded, their hearts full. Somehow, it felt just right. They leaned over to look once more at the baby, and then quietly turned back toward the hillside.

The lamb trotted happily beside them. And though they returned with their gift, they carried home something far more precious – **a memory they would treasure for the rest of their lives**.

The visit of the three kings, with gold, frankincense and myrrh

The three camel riders had managed to find their way to Jerusalem, and to their great delight when they knocked on the great door of the palace, which was thrown open by two guardsmen wielding great axes and shouting "Who is knocking on the kings gate?" they had been allowed in and then given permission to spend a few minutes with King Herod himself. Herod was dressed in a tunic embroidered with much gold thread, and he had a gold and silver headpiece that appeared to be covered in jewels, which shone brightly in the candlelight. To begin with Herod was quite courteous towards them and offered them a drink out of gold goblets, but once they had told him that they believed a new king had been born somewhere in his country he had very fiercely shouted insults at them. Then he gesticulated at them with his sword with great gusto and, ordering his guards to chase them out of the palace, he sent the three of them packing.

They left his palace with their tails between their legs, got onto their camels, and headed for the open country outside Jerusalem. To their great delight the amazingly bright star in the sky, which they thought had led them to Jerusalem, seemed to be leading them yet further on their journey, and so they followed it in the direction that it set… And after a few days it became stationary in the sky, right over Bethlehem.

"This is not a big town," said the rider of the leading camel, "but it's big enough to make a search confusing. Where do we start looking for a new baby."

The visit of the three kings, with gold, frankincense and myrrh

"There's an inn just over there," said one of his companions. "Let's go and have a flagon of wine each and ask if they have heard anything about this birth. The very least that we can do is allow us to bed down there for the night, and we can ask if the camels can use the stables, if they have any.

Just a few minutes later, they had tethered their camels onto the rail outside the inn and were inside sipping their wine.

"Now, Landlord," said Abednigo, "we are searching for a new-born baby. Have you heard of any being born in this town in the last couple of days. It is pretty important because we are told that there is a baby somewhere near here who is destined to become a king."

The landlord looked at them with astonishment.

"Well," he said, "that's fantastic. Two people turned up on their donkey begging for a room for the night because the man claimed that his wife was about to give birth. Because all my rooms were full I told them that they could stay overnight in my stable. A baby was born there just a couple of nights ago. And there have been some very strange goings on ever since. But his parents... well his parents couldn't look less the mother and father of a king. So I think that you had better head to the South end of the town and look in the posh part of this large village, or even in Bethsaida, which is quite a few miles away, but has some very wealthy people living there."

"Thanks for that! We'll be on our way in the morning quite early, and we'll head for Bethsaida if you can point us in the right direction. That said, we need to check out the baby in the stable here. You never know. Strange things happen. You just never know…"

Downing the last dregs of their flagons of wine, the three camel riders headed up to their bedroom and collected three parcels from their luggage.

Gold.

Frankincense

Myrrh

"Yes here are our gifts. They are all still fine, and not in any way broken or damaged. Fit for a king – if we can find him."

Just five minutes later they were all in the stable and were on bended knee in front of the crib that contained baby Jesus, with his parents standing behind them, looking on in great surprise. Without any warning Abednigo began to say a prayer.

"Lord, what a beautiful baby you have sent to us. Thank you. Your star that has lead us here. It tells us that he is destined to become a king. Bless these gifts that we have brought for him. They are gifts of gold, frankincense, and myrrh."

The visit of the three kings, with gold, frankincense and myrrh

"Good heavens," exclaimed Joseph, the baby's father. "What does he need those for?"

"Well," Joseph continued, "if you insist I suppose that just in case he is going to be king, we can take the frankincense and myrrh home with us, and my wife can save them for him for when he becomes an adult and understands their significance. But *gold*... why should he need gold? I am the best carpenter of the village where we live, and I have a lot of very good customers. They pay me very well. We have all the money that we need. Money for food, for wine, even to buy a new house if we decided to move away from our beautiful home by the river.

"So," Joseph looked the camel riders in the eyes and then continued, "give me the gold, and when the sun rises I am going to go down into Bethlehem and give this gold to the town's charity chairman. I am sure that he will find a good use for it. What is more, it will be the first thing that this baby king has done to change the lives of the poor who live hereabouts... which is something that I hope that he will continue to do all his life."

The three camel riders were upset. They had spent eighteen days travelling across the desert from their home lands to find this new king. Now one of the gifts that they had brought had been rejected. How ungrateful was that!

Thank goodness they had booked bedrooms in the inn for the next few nights. They needed to relax before making the long journey home again. The thought of having to cross that immense desert was extremely off-putting.

"Come on," said Abednigo. "We have spent enough time here. Why don't we go and put our things in our bedrooms at the inn. Then let's have a good supper and flagon of wine. I'm starving!"

Slightly-Nightly the Nightingale Sings a Lullaby

High above the stable, tucked deep in the shadows of the wooden roof, a small bird stirred on his perch. He was a **nightingale** – a beautiful one – with soft brown feathers, a tiny bright eye, and a voice so lovely it could bring people to tears. His name, rather fittingly, was **Slightly-Nightly**, because while most birds sang in the day, he preferred to sing just as the stars came out.

Usually, he lived in the treetops outside Bethlehem, hopping from branch to branch, filling the sky with his lilting, magical song. People in the village would often stop and listen, whispering to one another:

"That must be a nightingale! How lucky we are to hear it."

But just a few days ago, Slightly-Nightly had caught a **cold**. His eyes were puffy, and his wings felt tired. He couldn't see very well and flying between trees had become difficult.

One afternoon, searching for a place to rest, he spotted what he thought was a **hollow in an old oak tree** – just the kind of place he liked to hide away in when he wasn't feeling well. He flew straight into the opening… only to discover that it wasn't a tree at all! It was the **door-frame of an old timber barn**, part of the inn on the edge of Bethlehem.

Inside, it was dry and quiet. Slightly-Nightly was too tired to find a way out again, so he decided to stay right where he was – just for a little while – until he felt better. But then something strange happened.

He heard **crying**.

Not chirping. Not bleating. Not mooing.

Crying.

And it wasn't the cry of a lamb or calf. This was something else.

"Is that… a human baby?" Slightly-Nightly wondered.

Carefully, he fluttered down from the beam and glided low across the stable. The hay rustled beneath his wings as he flew, his poor eyes still blurry, but sharp enough to make out a **wooden crib** in the corner of an old animal stall. And inside it – **a baby**.

A new-born, red-faced and crying, his little fists clenched tight. The child looked so small, so new to the world. Slightly-Nightly tilted his head.

"A baby… in a stable? That's not where human babies usually sleep."

But then he remembered something important. People loved his **song**. They would stop to listen in the woods or smile when they heard him from their windows. He had often overheard them say:

"It's the nightingale! The most beautiful voice in all the world."

Suddenly, he had an idea.

"Maybe," he whispered, **"if I sing to the baby, I can help him stop crying… and go to sleep."**

He fluttered gently back to a high wooden beam near the ceiling and tucked his wings close. From there, he opened his beak – and began to sing. He sang softly at first – **long, fluting notes**, each one rising and falling like waves in the wind. The melody shimmered in the air, echoing off the wooden walls and wrapping the stable in sound.

Then came the magic. The baby stopped crying.

His fists relaxed. His eyelids fluttered.

And soon… he was asleep.

Slightly-Nightly smiled to himself.

"That's better," he thought. **"He just needed a lullaby."**

From that night on, whenever the baby stirred or cried, Slightly-Nightly would perch above the manger and sing his song – soft, warm, and full of love. And though no one ever saw him clearly, Mary would sometimes say:

"Do you hear that? That beautiful sound... It always starts just as Jesus begins to cry, and it always helps him sleep."

Joseph would nod and listen, eyes wide.

"It's a miracle," he'd whisper.

But up in the rafters, the little nightingale just kept singing, content to give the gift only **he** could offer – the gift of peace and comfort, carried on a song.

Bundle-Some the Talking Budgie Warns the King

Just down the road from the busy Bethlehem inn lived a cheerful Egyptian family – a mother, a father, and their three lively sons: **Luke**, **Lionel**, and **Lancer**.

Each of the boys had a pet.

Luke had a sturdy donkey named **Daniel**, whom he fed and cleaned up after every day. On weekends, Luke would ride Daniel through the winding streets and up into the hills, sometimes with a picnic tucked under his arm. Lionel had a long, gentle rat snake named **Serpentine**, who liked to curl lazily around his legs or waist like a silk belt. But the youngest boy, Lancer, had the most unusual pet of all – a bright green and yellow **budgerigar** named **Bundle-Some**.

Bundle-Some wasn't just any budgie. He **talked** – and not just a little. Thanks to Lancer's patient teaching, Bundle-Some could speak **fluent Hebrew**. His chirps had turned into clear, cheeky phrases, and he had a fondness for repeating whatever Lancer said.

He lived in a clever little cage made from dried bullrushes that Lancer's father had crafted. Most days, Lancer would let him out into the garden, holding corn in the palm of his hand so Bundle-Some would always return to rest and snack.

On this hot evening, Lancer decided his feathered friend could use some air. He filled his tunic pocket with fresh corn from the shed, opened the cage door and said gently, **"Come on, Bundle-Some. Let's go outside so you can fly."**

"Fly outside! Fly outside! Fly outside!" chirped the bird happily, fluttering from the cage and landing on Lancer's head.

As soon as they stepped into the sunlit yard, Bundle-Some took off. He soared high into the air, wheeled in a wide circle – and then, without warning, **vanished from sight**. He had heard something. A melody, soft and sweet, floating from the open barn door nearby.

It was **Slightly-Nightly**, the nightingale, singing his lullaby to the baby lying in the manger. Bundle-Some followed the sound, darted past the stable door, and flew in a loop around the rafters. But as he listened more closely, he heard not just music – but **voices**.

Three men, tall and well-dressed, stood around the crib. They spoke in hushed, awed tones:

"He is the child the stars spoke of," one said.

"The king who will lead the whole world," said another.

"He has been born here, in this stable, in Bethlehem."

Bundle-Some's little heart fluttered.

A king? A new king… right here?

And then Bundle-Some remembered something very important. He had been born in **King Herod's palace**. The palace maids had raised him after his mother, **Blossom**, had mysteriously disappeared. They had fed him, kept him warm, and taught him to perch and play.

"King Herod must be told," Bundle-Some thought. **"If there's a new king, he'll want to know. He might be in danger!"**

Without hesitation, the budgerigar zipped back into the sky. His wings beat fast as he soared over rooftops, past watchtowers and palm trees, flying straight toward the palace he had once called home.

He had one mission: **to deliver a warning**.

Bundle-Some knew just what he would do. He would land where all could see him – perhaps on the edge of Herod's throne – and cry out in the clearest voice he had:

"New king! New king! Baby in the barn! Baby in the barn!"

He would speak the truth. And he believed that King Herod would listen.

The Innkeeper Offers a Room

The morning sunlight filtered through the wooden slats of the stable roof as **Joseph** sat beside Mary, gently rocking their sleeping baby in his arms. He coughed – **a loud, scratchy cough** – and Mary looked at him with concern.

Joseph gave her a tired smile.

"I think it's time to go home," he said softly. **"This stable has been a blessing, but it's not the right place for our son… and this cough of mine won't get any better out here."**

Mary nodded.

"I agree," she said. **"I've got so much washing to do. New-borns are messy, and poor Matthias the innkeeper has already let me use his kitchen twice to scrub out the baby's diapers. I'll be glad to be home again."**

Joseph stood and stretched.

"Well, let me check on Dawnlight. I took her for a trot yesterday and her front leg seemed sore. I've rubbed in some ointment, so hopefully she's up to carrying you and the baby all the way back to Nazareth. But there's one more thing I

must do before we leave – register with the Roman centurion. That's the whole reason we came here in the first place."

Just then, the **stable door creaked open**. Framed in the light stood **Matthias** the innkeeper – kind-eyed and wearing a well-worn wool tunic. Though he had sent food to them during their stay, this was the first time he had come in person.

Joseph and Mary looked up in surprise.

"Good morning," Matthias said. "I see you're packing. But I've come to let you know – **you don't need to go just yet."**

Mary raised her eyebrows.

"Oh?"

"Yes," said Matthias, stepping no further than the doorway. **"Four of our guests have left for Cairo this morning. That means we have spare rooms now – and if you'd like, I can offer you a bedroom in the inn for the next few nights. Fresh sheets, a real bed, and no straw in your shoes."**

Mary smiled kindly.

"That's a very generous offer. But I think we'll still go home. We want the baby to begin his life where he truly belongs. And though our neighbours are watching the house, it's best if we're there ourselves."

Matthias nodded but didn't step inside.

"**Suit yourselves,**" he said. "**But it's a long journey for a new-born. If you change your mind, you're welcome to come over. I'll only charge you five shekels a night – half the usual price, as long as you don't stay more than three nights.**"

Joseph and Mary thanked him warmly. Then, with a quick nod and a soft smile, the innkeeper **turned on his heel and disappeared**, the door swinging gently behind him. Mary and Joseph looked at one another, then down at their sleeping son.

"**He'll be just fine,**" Mary whispered.

Outside, the wind whispered too, as if agreeing.

Sonia and the Precious Pearl

Just down the dusty street from the inn in Bethlehem stood a small, crumbling shack. It leaned slightly to one side, its roof was patched with old straw, and the wooden door creaked every time the wind blew. To most, it didn't look like a home at all – but inside it lived a mother and her little girl.

The mother's name was **Georgina**, and her four-year-old daughter was called **Sonia**. They hadn't always lived in that broken-down house. A few years ago, Georgina's husband had gone off to fight in the Roman army and never returned. Without his letters or the money he used to send home, life had grown very hard. They lost their house, and it seemed as though they might lose everything else too.

But Georgina's kind boss at the mill gave her the little shack to live in – for free. It wasn't much, but it was safe and dry, and they were together. That was what mattered most. One warm afternoon, Sonia woke from her nap, rubbed her sleepy eyes, and wandered into the kitchen, where her mother was kneading bread dough by the window.

"Mummy," said Sonia, her big eyes shining, **"the children at Number Three say a baby was born at the inn last night! Is that true? But I don't think Miriam, the innkeeper's wife, was having a baby..."**

Georgina smiled softly.

"**It wasn't Miriam,**" she said. "**It was a woman from far away. A couple from Nazareth arrived very late. The woman was riding on a donkey, and when they got here, she started having pains – so they knew the baby was coming. But the town was packed. No one had any rooms left. The man tried everywhere – even offered a king's ransom – but no one could take them in. In the end, the innkeeper let them stay in the stable. And that's where their baby was born.**"

Sonia's mouth dropped open.

"**In the stable? With the animals?**"

"**Yes,**" said her mother, nodding. "**And they named him Jesus. People say he's very special. That he's going to be a king one day. Some wealthy travellers came on camels from far away – Arabia, I think – just to see him. They followed a star in the sky, and the star led them here.**"

Sonia's eyes sparkled.

"**Mummy! That's amazing! I want to go and see him. Please, can I?**"

Before Georgina could answer, Sonia was already skipping toward her tiny bedroom.

"**I'm going to bring him a present!**" she called. "**The most precious thing I own.**"

She returned moments later, holding a tiny cloth bundle in her hands. She unwrapped it carefully to reveal a small, shimmering **pearl**.

"You gave this to me, remember?" she said. **"You found it inside an oyster when you went swimming in the Red Sea. You said it was a treasure, and I've kept it very safe. But now I want to give it to baby Jesus. If he's going to be a king one day, I want him to have my pearl. He'll know I gave it from my heart."**

Georgina's eyes filled with tears. She didn't say no. Hand in hand, they walked down the road towards the inn. And just outside the stable, as stars began to twinkle overhead, little Sonia stepped inside, her pearl tucked in her palm, ready to give her treasure to the baby lying in the manger.

The Innkeeper's Wife Brings a Gift

In the warm kitchen of the inn, **Miriam**, the innkeeper's wife, was busy arranging bowls and tidying up after the morning's guests. She had just heard the front door creak and turned to see a little girl standing shyly by the counter. It was **Sonia**, the child who lived in the run-down house next door.

"May I please go see the baby in your stable?" Sonia had asked sweetly. **"I want to give him a gift."**

Miriam smiled and nodded at once.

"Of course you may. How kind of you to think of the baby."

But as Sonia disappeared out the door, Miriam paused and looked out across the courtyard toward the stable. Then a sudden thought came over her, and her cheeks turned pink.

"I haven't even gone to see the baby myself!" she said aloud. **"He was born in our stable – in our home, really – and I haven't even said hello."**

She felt a flutter in her chest. **A little girl had thought to bring a gift… but not the innkeeper's own wife.**

"I must make that right," Miriam whispered. **"I'll cook something for them. Something warm and comforting."**

She tied on her apron, lit the courtyard fire, and began to peel some apples from the fruit store. Into her big black pot went apples, a trickle of honey, a pinch of spice. Soon, the smell of simmering apple stew floated through the air. While the fruit bubbled gently, Miriam went to the cupboard and retrieved a skin of fresh milk.

Milk and stew. Good, thoughtful gifts. But somehow, **they didn't feel like enough**. As she stirred the pot, she looked down at her wrist – and saw the silver **bangle** she always wore. It had been a gift from **Matthias** the innkeeper, given to her one year after they had been betrothed. She gently slid it off.

"Yes," she said to herself. **"This is what I must give – not to the baby, but to his mother."**

She thought about Mary. So young. So far from home. She had travelled all this way on a donkey, knowing her baby might come at any time. She had no bed to give birth in. No midwife to help her. No warm house to rest in. And yet, she had done it.

"She deserves something precious," Miriam said, tucking the bangle into her apron pocket.

She lifted the stew from the fire, cradled the milk, and stepped out into the cool morning, crossing the dusty yard toward the stable.

Inside, it was dim and peaceful. In the stall where the innkeeper's bull used to sleep, **Mary sat quietly**, holding her baby close as he nursed.

"Mary," Miriam whispered, stepping gently inside. **"What a beautiful baby. I've heard his name is Jesus. A perfect name."**

Mary smiled and nodded. She looked tired – but calm. Happy.

"I've brought you something," Miriam continued. **"Not for the baby – he's already had so many visitors and gifts – but for you."**

She placed the pot of apple stew down beside the manger.

"Here's a sweet stew made from our own apples, and a skin of milk if you need it."

Then, Miriam reached into her apron and brought out the **bangle**.

"But this – this is for you."

She slipped the silver bracelet gently over Mary's wrist.

"This was a gift to me once, from someone I love very much. Now I give it to you – because this place, this stable, is where something truly precious happened.

And every time you look at this bangle, I hope it reminds you… that in the very spot you sit now, a miracle was born."

Mary's eyes filled with tears.

"Thank you," she whispered. **"I will treasure it always."**

And in that quiet moment, the two women – so different, and yet suddenly so close – sat together beside the child who would change the world.

Everybody Comes to the Stable

It was very late in the night, and the stable was still. A soft wind whispered through the cracks in the wooden walls, and the stars blinked gently overhead.

Mary, tired from the long journey and the days after her baby's birth, lay on a bed of straw next to the crib where **Jesus** slept. Though the straw had been piled high to make the floor soft, it was still not as comfortable as a real bed.

But Mary didn't notice. She was already fast asleep. And she was dreaming.

Joseph, sitting nearby, watched over her. He could hear her murmuring in her sleep.

"Who are you?" she whispered. **"Why are you here? You say your name is… 'Everybody'? What a strange name…"**

Joseph leaned forward, puzzled.

"You've brought the baby a present?"

Mary's face moved gently as she dreamed, her lips forming the words.

"It's time for you to leave," she mumbled.

Joseph was concerned. There was no one else in the stable. Only the two of them and the sleeping child. Should he wake her? But before he could move, Mary's eyes opened.

"Where is Everybody?" she asked softly.

Joseph blinked.

"Who?"

"Everybody," said Mary, sitting up. **"She was just here. A girl, about ten years old. She came to see Jesus in my dream."**

Joseph gave her a gentle smile.

"There's no one else here, my love. Just you, me, and the baby. You must have had a dream, that's all."

Mary nodded slowly.

"Yes, I know. But it didn't feel like a dream. She felt real. And so did her mother. They told me the story of how she got her name."

Joseph listened quietly.

"**Her mother told her,**" Mary continued, "**that she had always believed a child would be born one day who would become king of the whole world – not with power and armies, but with love and peace. A king who would change the world with kindness.**"

"**So,**" Mary said softly, "**she named her daughter *Everybody*. Because she believed that one day, Everybody would go to find this baby king – and that when she did, she would carry the hopes and hearts of all the people in the world.**"

Joseph said nothing. The stable seemed even quieter now.

"**And then,**" Mary whispered, "Everybody cried. She said, 'I've been given the most important job in the world. I'm going to find the baby, and when I do, I will tell him... that Everybody loves him, and Everybody always will.'"

Mary looked down at her baby boy, his tiny chest rising and falling as he slept.

"**It was only a dream,**" she said, "**but somehow, it felt like a promise.**"

And Joseph knew, as he watched his son sleeping beneath the stars, that **one day, that promise would come true**. Because someday, somewhere, in their own way... **Everybody** would come to the stable.

Wallie the Wolf Makes a Vow

Late one night, in the quiet of the stable, **Mary** stirred and whispered to Joseph:

"Did you hear that? It sounded like… wolves."

Joseph listened. Far off in the hills above Bethlehem, a soft, eerie howling echoed through the valley. He nodded.

"Yes. I've heard that before – back in Nazareth. They're far away, but I agree… it's a little frightening."

Up in the hills, hidden among the tall trees and shadows, a strong and clever wolf named **Wallie** stood at the head of his pack. He was the leader of twelve wolves, and tonight he had a plan.

"Listen carefully," Wallie told the others. **"Tonight, we hunt. I've heard there are animals in the town below. We'll move quietly – no howling, no noise. We stay in the shadows and follow the river wall. That way, no one will see us."**

The pack followed him in perfect silence, moving like mist down the hillside. They stayed hidden behind the stone wall near the river, then padded along the edge of town. The

inn was just ahead. That's when Wallie heard something. It was the voice of **Miriam**, the innkeeper's wife. She was talking to someone inside the inn.

"I begged them to stay," Miriam said. **"I even offered supper for free. But Mary said no. She and Joseph are going home. They're leaving with the baby at daybreak."**

Wallie paused.

"The baby...?" he whispered to himself.

He listened more closely.

"They say that child," Miriam continued, **"is to be king – not just of people, but of the whole world. Even the animals. He will teach peace. He will bring light."**

Wallie's heart pounded.

A king? A king who will care for everyone? For animals too?

Then he thought something terrible.

"What if something happens to him?" Wallie murmured. **"What if he's attacked... hurt... even killed?"**

He turned to his pack.

"We're not going hunting tonight," he growled. **"We're going home. We have a mission far more important than finding food."**

The wolves raced silently back to the forest and gathered at the den. Wallie stood tall and proud.

"We will protect that child," he told them. **"Tomorrow, Mary and Joseph will leave. We'll follow them – quietly, from the hills. They must never see us. They must never know we're there. But we will guard them as far as our land allows."**

He turned to two of his best scouts.

"Wango. Wackbert. You're swift and silent. Go to the inn and keep watch. When they leave, come tell me. We'll be ready."

Wango and Wackbert raced off into the night. They waited quietly on a hill above the inn. For seven hours, they didn't move. Then, just as the **sun rose**, the stable door opened.

Joseph led the donkey, **Dawnlight**, onto the road. On her back sat Mary, with baby Jesus wrapped in a carry-blanket across her chest. The donkey's panniers were packed with clothes and blankets. The moment the little family stepped onto the road, the scouts ran to alert the pack.

And so, for **ten whole hours**, the wolves followed them. They ran through forests, behind rocks, and through long grass, always watching. Always ready. Then, just as **evening fell**, a young fox leapt from the bushes. One of the youngest wolves, **Wilwolf**, was startled – and let out a loud **howl**.

Down on the road, Joseph stiffened.

"Wolves," he whispered. **"Hold tight, Mary. I see lights ahead. That must be the inn where we'll stop for the night."**

He urged Dawnlight forward, walking as fast as they could. But Joseph didn't know the truth. Wallie had heard the howl too. And he wasn't angry – just understanding.

"Wilwolf," he said gently, **"you're still learning. But this time, it's time to go."**

Then, just as he promised, Wallie stood tall on his back legs, raised his head, and let out the softest bark:

"Woof… woof… woof…"

And the entire wolf pack turned quietly around… and ran back home to the hills.

The baby king was safe.

Osbert the Wise Owl Watches Over the Stable

High in the ancient oak tree beside the stable, just where the thickest branches met the sky, lived **Osbert**, a wise and rather serious **barn owl**. He had lived there for many years, longer than most of the birds and creatures nearby. His wide golden eyes had seen many things – quiet winters, stormy summers, sleepy donkeys, clucking chickens, even the occasional fox sneaking through the shadows. But nothing – **nothing at all** – had ever been quite like the last few days.

"Hoo," he muttered softly to himself as he peered down at the stable below. **"So many visitors. So much noise."**

First there were the parents – Mary and Joseph – arriving with their donkey in the middle of the night. Then came shepherds with woolly cloaks, talking about angels and stars. Later, there were camels with men in fancy robes carrying shiny gifts. There had even been a talking budgerigar, a dancing bat, and a very determined blackbird weaving reeds into the roof.

It had been fascinating… but also **terribly inconvenient**.

"I usually hunt near the barn," Osbert grumbled, **"but there hasn't been a moment's peace. I had to fly all the way to the far end of town just to catch one mouse!"**

Still, he couldn't help but feel that something important – **very important** – had happened down below in that humble stable. Something bigger than even his wise old owl-mind could quite understand. Tonight, perched quietly on his branch, Osbert heard Joseph's voice rising gently from inside the stable.

"We're nearly packed," Joseph said to Mary. **"Dawnlight the donkey is rested, and the baby is sleeping. It's time to go home."**

Osbert blinked.

"So they're leaving," he whispered. **"At last."**

And yet... he felt something strange.

Sadness?

Yes. Just a little.

He had grown used to hearing the baby's cries in the night, and Mary's soft singing. He had enjoyed watching the animals come and go with their curious gifts – logs, wool, reeds, milk, even warm duck down. He had even begun to feel that, somehow, **he had been part of it all too**, even though he hadn't gone into the stable himself.

Suddenly, Osbert stood up tall on his branch.

"I may not have given anything," he said, **"but I have watched over this family every night. I have kept guard with my eyes wide open. And perhaps that is my gift."**

He puffed out his chest feathers and looked proudly down at the little stable one last time. Then, spreading his great wings wide, **Osbert soared into the sky**, flying a wide, gentle circle over the stable.

"Farewell, baby Jesus," he whispered into the wind. **"I will remember you always."**

And as dawn broke over Bethlehem, the owl's shadow passed silently across the hills… just as the Holy Family set off for home.

Homeward Bound

By the time the sun had risen high into the sky, it was nearly **coffee time – 11 o'clock in the morning** – and **Mary and Joseph** had finished packing their few belongings. The stable was now quiet, the animals watching curiously as the family prepared to leave. **Baby Jesus** was fast asleep, so Joseph carefully wrapped him in his soft carry-cloth and gently helped Mary slide the sling over her shoulders. Together they stepped out into the daylight, where **Dawnlight the Donkey** stood waiting patiently.

Joseph reached into his satchel and took out a **fresh orange carrot** – one of six they had been saving. He held it out, and Dawnlight crunched it happily between her teeth. The other five carrots were tucked away into a saddlebag for treats later on the journey.

"Kneel," Joseph commanded gently, and at once, Dawnlight dropped her front legs and bowed her head. Joseph had trained her well. She stayed perfectly still while Mary climbed onto her back and settled into her **side-saddle position**, the baby nestled securely in her arms.

A moment later, they were on their way – **through the inn gate and out into the road**, heading north toward Nazareth.

"I'm so excited," Mary said softly, as the town of Bethlehem grew smaller behind them. **"Most of all, I can't wait to see my cousin Elizabeth again. She'll be amazed

when she sees baby Jesus. And just wait till I tell her about all the visitors we had!"

Her voice danced with energy as she remembered.

"The shepherds, the lamb they brought… the camel riders from the East with their gifts of frankincense, myrrh, and gold." She sighed. **"I do wish you had let me keep the gold. We could've used it for Jesus' schooling. He could grow up to be a scholar, Joseph. Maybe even a teacher!"**

Joseph didn't answer.

He was watching the road carefully, focused on guiding Dawnlight over the uneven, **stony path**. The hills were steep here, and one wrong step could be dangerous. Mary noticed his silence.

"Do you know where we'll sleep tonight?" she asked gently. **"Or are we going to end up in another stable?"**

Joseph looked back over his shoulder, his brow furrowed with worry.

"Trust me," he said, trying to sound calm even as stress crept into his voice. **"Keeping you and the baby safe is my first priority. We'll stop well before it gets dark, and I'll find us a good place to rest. Somewhere warm. Somewhere safe. We'll have a meal, and then we'll sleep. I promise."**

Mary smiled and reached down to pat Dawnlight's neck. The donkey walked on, her ears twitching as birds chirped in the olive trees overhead.

And so the Holy Family made their way home – **a baby, a mother, a father, and a donkey**, walking slowly under the wide blue sky, with the weight of the world gently cradled in Mary's arms.

Cassidy the Cockerel Crows the Alarm

Cassidy the Cockerel was a proud and handsome bird, with a shiny scarlet comb, a golden beak, and tail feathers that shimmered blue, green, and black in the sunlight. He lived in a sunny field on the edge of **Bethlehem**, where he ruled over a happy group of eighteen clucking hens.

His owner, **Sansorino**, was a kind farmer who loved his animals. Every morning, before breakfast, he would carry a great silver bucket of grain into the field and scatter it generously on the grass. This morning was no different. Cassidy had had his breakfast early and was now perched on his favourite branch high in an **orange tree** at the corner of the field near the village bakery. The warm breeze rustled the leaves, and the scent of baking bread filled the air.

But then... **something strange happened**.

From his high perch, Cassidy spotted a group of **soldiers** marching swiftly into the town. Their swords flashed. Their leader was barking orders.

"No time to wait! Go into every house!" the soldier shouted. **"The king's orders are clear – no baby boys under two are to be left in Bethlehem!"**

Cassidy's feathers bristled.

"What? Take the babies? What sort of king would do such a thing?"

His heart raced. He had seen many babies in Bethlehem, including the one born just days ago in the **stable near the inn**. That baby had been visited by shepherds and wise men… everyone said he was someone special.

"I must do something!" Cassidy squawked. And then he had an idea.

He spread his wings wide, flapped hard, and launched himself from the tree. As he flew over the rooftops, he began to **crow** as loudly as he possibly could:

"COCK-A-DOODLE-DOO! COCK-A-DOODLE-DOO!!"

He swooped over **Lake Street**, cawing. Then down **Desert Road**, again and again. Then over **Inn Terrace** and across the **Town Square**.

"COCK-A-DOODLE-DOO!!"

People opened their windows. Shopkeepers paused. Mothers clutched their babies and looked toward the sky. Cassidy didn't know if they understood him – but he hoped they did.

He flew for hours, shouting his alarm over the town, his throat growing sore. Then, near the bakery, a man burst from a house – **Mohammed the Blacksmith**.

"The king's soldiers!" Mohammed screamed. **"They came into my house! They tried to take my baby boy – but he wasn't there. My wife had taken him out. I had to bribe them with silver coins to get them to leave!"**

Neighbours rushed outside. The word spread like fire.

"They're heading to the inn!" Mohammed shouted. **"I have to warn them!"**

Cassidy soared above him, still crowing as loud as he could.

"COCK-A-DOODLE-DOO!"

At last, Mohammed reached the inn and shouted the news. The innkeeper, startled, held up his hands.

"The baby born here is gone," he said with relief. **"His parents left with their donkey early this morning. They're long gone. Thank goodness!"**

Cassidy fluttered down to the inn's rooftop, listening closely. He gave one final crow of triumph.

"COCK-A-DOODLE-DOOOOOOOO!"

He had done it. His voice had helped spread the warning.

He had helped **save lives**.

As the sun dipped low in the sky, Cassidy flew back to his orange tree, tired but proud. His chest puffed out. His feathers glowed in the golden light. And though he didn't know it, his voice that day had echoed far and wide, and **his courage had made a difference**.

Constance, Constantinople, and Canonfire: The Urgent Escape

Three tall, elegant **camels** stood quietly beside the inn, their reins loosely tied to a wooden fence. Their names were **Constance**, **Constantinople**, and **Canonfire** – three of the finest camels in the Eastern desert, chosen specially to carry their wise and wealthy masters on an important mission.

They had travelled far – across sands and valleys, rivers and rocks – all to bring their **three kings** to Bethlehem to meet a very special baby.

But now the air in the town had changed. They could feel it in the wind. They could hear it in the panic of voices on the street. They could see it in the flapping wings of **Cassidy the cockerel**, who was flying over rooftops, **crowing with all his might.**

"Something's wrong," said Constance, flattening her ears.

"I agree," said Constantinople. **"There's shouting coming from every corner of the village. And the innkeeper just yelled at a soldier. I think there's danger."**

Canonfire stamped her hooves.

"**But our kings are inside the inn. They've been resting for two days. The guests left, and they were offered lovely rooms. They won't know anything about what's happening outside!**"

Constance nodded.

"**Do you remember what King Herod said when we visited his palace?**" she asked. "**He told our masters that if they found the baby, they must return and tell him. But they didn't. They followed the star here – but they never went back.**"

"**Then Herod might be furious!**" gasped Canonfire. "**He might send his soldiers to capture them!**"

"**We have to warn them,**" said Constantinople. "**We must get them out of here before it's too late!**"

The camels thought hard.

"**Let's bray as loud as we can!**" Canonfire suggested.

"**No,**" said Constance, shaking her head. "**They'll just think we're hungry. It has to be something big. Something that gets their attention at once.**"

They looked around. And then they saw it.

A **fence** to their left... A large **water butt** to their right.

"Let's make a mess!" said Constantinople.

"YES!" cried the others.

The three camels reared up on their hind legs and **kicked with all their might**. With a crash and a crack, the fence splintered and collapsed to the ground. The water butt gave way with a mighty splash, sending water pouring into the dusty street. Inside the inn, **the innkeeper** dropped his spoon mid-sip.

"Those blasted camels!" he shouted. **"They're destroying everything! I'm going to find their owners and get them OUT!"**

The camels listened, holding their breath.

CRASH! The inn doors burst open, and their three kings – each carrying their royal packs – rushed outside.

"What on Earth is happening?" one cried.

"Mount up!" shouted another. **"Let's ride – NOW!"**

Without waiting for another word, the kings leapt onto the backs of their camels. With a flick of the reins and a **thump of the saddle**, they were galloping down the street, **sand**

and dust flying behind them, their robes billowing in the breeze. **And they never looked back.**

As the camels thundered out of Bethlehem, they knew they had done the right thing. They had **saved their masters** from Herod's wrath, just in time. And somewhere out in the quiet hills, a cockerel let out one last proud **cock-a-doodle-doo** – a salute to his fellow heroes with humps.

www.ingramcontent.com/pod-product-compliance
Lightning Source LLC
Chambersburg PA
CBHW061149070526
44584CB00034B/4464